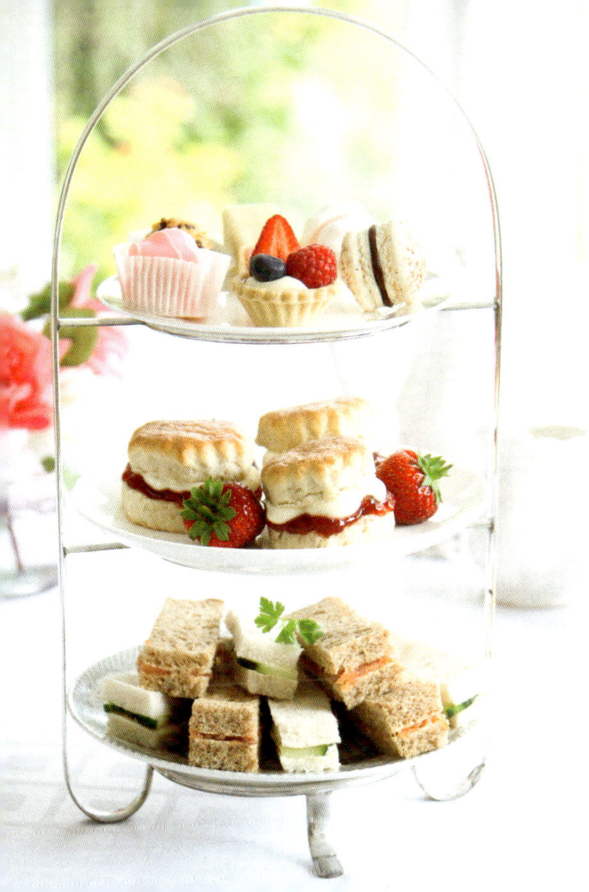

AF085295

Favourite English Teatime Recipes

Traditional cakes from around the shires

Illustrated with true British pictures

Index

Banbury Cakes 42
Bath Buns 39
Belvoir Castle Buns 27
Brighton Gingerbread 46
Bury Simnel Cake 43
Chelsea Buns 7
Cornish Saffron Cake 3
Coventry Godcakes 22
Cranham Honey Cake 10
Derbyshire Chocolate Cake 5
Devonshire Apple Scones 6
Devonshire Cider Cake 45
Gloucester Tartlets 40
Hampshire Picnic Cake 15
Hereford Brandy Snaps 24
Isle of Wight Farmhouse Cake 18
Kentish Cob-nut Cake 32
Lakeland Lemon Cake 16
Leamingtons 19
Norfolk Vinegar Cake 29
Northamptonshire Seed Cake 12
Nottingham Coffee Biscuits 30
Old Harry Rock Cakes 38
Richmond Maids of Honour 11
Shropshire Lambing Cake 35
South Tyne Yeast Cake 31
Spiced Oxford Cake 23
Staffordshire Fruit Cake 47
Suffolk 'Fourses' Cake 8
Surrey Lardie Cakes 21
Wiltshire White Cake 26
Windsor Castle Cake 34
Yorkshire Sticky Parkin 14
Yorkshire Tea Cakes 37

Back Cover: Bodiam Castle, Back Cover: Shanklin on the Isle of Wight
Title page: English tea selection

Printed & published by Dorrigo, Manchester, England © Copyright
All rights reserved. No part of this publication may be reproduced, stored in a retrieval system or transmitted, in any form or by means, electronic, mechanical, photocopying or otherwise. Images: Adobe Stock Images, Recipes: J Salmon Ltd.

Cornish Saffron Cake

This Old English cake or sweet bread which originated in Cornwall is made from saffron flavoured yeast dough with currants and candied peel. The high proportion of yeast is needed because the loaf is enriched with so much fat.

1 teaspoon saffron strands	6 oz butter
1-2 tablespoons boiling water	2 sachets 'easy-blend' yeast
1 lb strong flour	3 oz sugar
½ teaspoon salt	6 oz currants
½ teaspoon ground nutmeg	2 oz chopped candied peel

6 fl.oz lukewarm milk

Steep the saffron in the boiled water. Grease a 2 lb loaf tin. Sift the flour, salt and nutmeg into a bowl and rub in the butter until the mixture resembles breadcrumbs. Then add the yeast, sugar, currants and peel and mix well. Make a well in the mixture, add the saffron water and sufficient of the warm milk to produce a soft dough. Turn out on a floured surface and knead well for about 10 minutes. Put in a clean bowl, cover and leave in a warm place to rise; the heavy dough is somewhat slow to rise. When risen, knead again and put into the tin. Leave in the warm to prove. Set oven to 375°F or Mark 5. Bake for about 40 minutes then reduce oven to 350°F or Mark 4 and bake for about a further 50 minutes until a skewer inserted comes out clean. Leave to cool in the tin for 15 minutes then turn out on to a wire rack. Serve sliced and buttered.

Derbyshire Chocolate Cake

A chocolate sponge cake with chocolate filling and chocolate glacé icing.

3 oz drinking chocolate
4 oz self-raising flour
6 oz margarine
6 oz caster sugar
3 eggs, well beaten
1 tablespoon hot water
FILLING
2 oz margarine
2 oz drinking chocolate
4 oz icing sugar
Water or milk to mix, if required
GLACÉ ICING
6 oz icing sugar
2 oz drinking chocolate
Water to mix
(approx. 2 tablespoons)

Set oven to 350°F or Mark 4. Grease and line two 8 inch sandwich tins. Sieve together the flour and drinking chocolate. Cream the margarine and sugar together in a bowl until light and fluffy. Beat in the eggs, a little at a time, adding a tablespoon of the flour mixture to prevent curdling. Fold in the remaining flour and chocolate mixture and stir in the hot water. Put the mixture into the tins and smooth the tops. Bake for 25 minutes or until the surface springs back when pressed lightly. Remove the cakes from the tins and cool on a wire rack. Buttercream filling: mix all the ingredients together until smooth and light. Spread on one of the cakes and sandwich together. Icing: add the water to the sugar and the drinking chocolate to form a thick paste and coat the top of the cake before serving.

Canal boats at Shardlow Wharf

Devonshire Apple Scones

These rough-shaped, spicy scones look more like rock cakes than conventional scones and the chopped apple gives them a pleasant, moist texture.

8 oz wholemeal self-raising flour
1 teaspoon ground cinnamon
1 teaspoon baking powder
4 oz butter
2 oz soft brown sugar
2 medium sized cooking apples, peeled, cored and finely diced
1 medium egg

Set oven to 375F or Mark 5. Mix the flour, cinnamon and baking powder together in a large bowl. Rub in the butter, stir in the sugar and apple and lastly stir in the egg. Mould into 10 or 12 small, rough heaps (as you would for rock cakes) and place on a floured baking sheet. The mixture must not be too wet or the scones will lose their 'rocky' shape. Bake for 20-25 minutes. Allow to cool slightly before transferring to a wire rack. Serve split in half, with butter.

Chelsea Buns

This small, sweet yeast cake was an 18th century speciality of the Old Chelsea Bun House in Pimlico, then in the London Borough of Chelsea.

¼ pt warm milk less 3 tablespoons
2 level teaspoons dried yeast
½ teaspoon sugar
8 oz flour
½ teaspoon salt
1 egg, beaten
½ oz butter, melted

FILLING
½ oz melted butter
2 oz soft brown sugar
3 oz currants
½ oz mixed peel, chopped

Demerara sugar for glazing

In a warmed bowl blend the yeast with the milk, sugar and 2 oz of the flour. Leave in a warm place until frothy. Mix the salt with the remaining flour and stir into the yeast mixture with the egg and ½ oz melted butter. Mix well, turn out on to a floured surface and knead for 10 minutes. Cover and leave in a warm place to rise until doubled in bulk. Knead again and roll out a rectangle about 9 inches by 12 inches. Brush with ½ oz melted butter, evenly sprinkle on the brown sugar and dried fruit and press down. Roll up from the short edge, seal and cut into 9 slices about 1 inch thick. Grease a 7 inch square cake tin, arrange the slices, cut side up, in 3 x 3 rows and sprinkle tops with demerara sugar. Prove until risen and springy. Set oven to 375°F or Mark 5 and bake for about 25-30 minutes until brown. Turn out and cool on a rack before separating.

Suffolk 'Fourses' Cake

This currant bread was eaten by farm-workers in the fields at teatime, namely around 4 o'clock; hence the name.

1½ lb strong flour	2 teaspoons sugar
½ teaspoon salt	¾ pint warm water
2 teaspoons mixed spice	6 oz lard
½ oz fresh yeast	6 oz currants

Lightly grease two 1lb. loaf tins. Sift the flour, salt and spice together. Cream the yeast and sugar together with a little of the water and allow to sponge. In a bowl, rub the lard into the flour, make a well in the centre and add the yeast mixture. Stir in the remaining water to form a smooth dough. Turn out on to a lightly floured surface and knead thoroughly. Cover and leave to rise in a warm place until the dough has doubled in bulk. Knead again, adding the currants so that they are well distributed in the dough. Divide the dough into the tins. Cover and leave to prove in a warm place. Set oven to 400°F or Mark 6; when the dough has risen to about 1 inch above the top of the tins bake for 45 minutes. While still warm brush the tops of the loaves with a little water or milk to give a slight sheen. Serve plain or spread with butter.

High street Lavenham, Suffolk

Cranham Honey Cake

Large quantities of honey are made in Essex, of which this cake takes full advantage.

8 oz self-raising flour
2 eggs, beaten
5 oz margarine
2½ oz caster sugar
3 oz thick honey
Grated rind of a lemon
2 oz glacé cherries, chopped
Pinch of salt
4 tablespoons milk

Set oven to 375°F or Mark 5. Grease and flour a 7 inch round cake tin. Cream together in a bowl the margarine, sugar and honey. Beat the eggs and then beat them into the mixture. Fold in the sieved flour, salt, cherries and lemon rind. Add the milk and mix well. Turn into the tin and bake for one hour until golden brown. Allow to cool in the tin before turning out on to a wire rack.

Richmond Maids of Honour

This small tartlet originated in Henry VIII's palace of Hampton Court, where it was popular with the Queen's Maids of Honour. Later the secret recipe was made at a shop established at Richmond, Surrey.

8 oz puff pastry
8 oz ground almonds
4 oz caster sugar
2 eggs, beaten

1 oz flour
4 tablespoons double cream
Pinch ground nutmeg
2 teaspoons lemon juice

A little sifted icing sugar

Set oven to 400°F or Mark 6. Grease and flour 20 patty tins. Roll out the pastry on a lightly floured surface and use to line the tins, trimming the edges neatly. In a bowl, mix together the ground almonds and sugar, then stir in the beaten eggs, flour, cream, nutmeg and lemon juice. Divide the mixture between the pastry cases and bake for about 15 minutes or until firm and golden. Turn out on to a wire rack and allow to cool. Serve dredged with a little icing sugar.

Northamptonshire Seed Cake

A plain cake flavoured with nutmeg and caraway seeds, traditionally served at sheep shearing time.

8 oz butter
8 oz caster sugar
4 eggs
8 oz flour
½ teaspoon baking powder
1 teaspoon ground nutmeg
1 oz caraway seeds

Set oven to 350°F or Mark 4. Grease and line an 8 inch round cake tin. Cream the butter and sugar together in a bowl until light and fluffy. Place the eggs in a bowl set over a saucepan of hot water and whisk until fluffy, then whisk into the butter mixture. Sift the flour and baking powder together and fold into the mixture, together with the nutmeg. Add the caraway seeds and combine well. Turn into the prepared tin and smooth over the top. Bake for 1½-2 hours, covering the top with a piece of kitchen foil if it appears to be browning too quickly. Cool in the tin for 5 minutes, then turn out on to a wire rack.

Cat Bells - The Lake District

Yorkshire Sticky Parkin

This delicious cake was always served on Bonfire Night as well as other occasions. It is best kept in a tin for about a week before eating to allow it to become really moist; hence the name 'sticky'.

8 oz flour
2 level teaspoons baking powder
2 level teaspoons ground ginger
1 level teaspoon ground cinnamon
8 oz medium oatmeal

6 oz black treacle
4 oz margarine
6 oz soft brown sugar
1 egg, beaten
¼ pint milk

Set oven to 350°F or Mark 4. Grease and line with greaseproof paper the base and sides of a 9 inch square cake tin. Sieve the flour, baking powder, ginger and cinnamon into a large bowl and stir in the oatmeal. Put the treacle, margarine and soft brown sugar into a pan over a low heat and stir occasionally until the margarine has just melted. Make a well in the centre of the dry ingredients and gradually stir in the treacle mixture and then the egg and milk. Beat well until smooth. Pour into the tin and place in the oven for approximately one hour. Cool slightly in the tin and then turn on to a wire rack. Store in an airtight tin. Serve on its own or with butter.

Hampshire Picnic Cake

This lightly spiced honey and walnut fruit cake is from an old county recipe.

- **4 oz butter**
- **8 oz sugar**
- **3 eggs, beaten together**
- **6 oz flour**
- **½ teaspoon baking powder**
- **¼ teaspoon salt**
- **½ teaspoon ground nutmeg**
- **¼ teaspoon ground cinnamon**
- **2 tablespoons milk**
- **¼ teaspoon bicarbonate of soda**
- **2 tablespoons clear honey**
- **6 oz walnut kernels – 6 reserved for decoration, the rest roughly chopped**
- **6 oz raisins or sultanas**

Set oven to 325°F or Mark 3. Well grease and lightly flour a 2 lb loaf tin. Cream the butter and sugar together in a bowl until light and fluffy and beat in a little of the eggs. Sift the flour, baking powder, salt and spices together, then add alternately to the creamed mixture with the remainder of the eggs. Warm the milk slightly and stir in the honey, then add the bicarbonate of soda and stir into the mixture. Add the chopped nuts and dried fruit and combine well together. Spoon the mixture into the tin and bake for 1-1½ hours, covering the top with kitchen foil if it appears to be browning too quickly. Place the reserved walnuts on the top of the cake, and bake for a futher 40-45 minutes. Cool in the tin for 30 minutes, then turn out on to a wire rack.

Lakeland Lemon Cake

A spicy, lemon flavoured cake which can be eaten plain or sliced and filled with lemon curd.

8 oz self-raising flour	**Pinch of ground cinnamon**
6 oz butter	**½ level teaspoon ground ginger**
6 oz caster sugar	**Grated rind, and juice of**
2 large eggs, beaten	**1 large lemon**
Pinch of salt	**1 tablespoon milk**

Set oven to 325°F or Mark 3. Grease and line the base and sides of a 7 inch round cake tin. In a bowl, cream the butter and sugar until pale and fluffy. Add the beaten eggs, salt, cinnamon and ginger, sieve in the flour and mix well. Add the lemon rind and juice and then add the milk. Mix well and place in the prepared tin. Level the top and bake for about 1 hour until firm and pale brown. Leave in the tin for 15 minutes and then transfer to a wire rack. Keep for 48 hours before cutting. Serve either plain or cut in half and sandwiched with home-made lemon curd.

Isle of Wight Farmhouse Cake

A straight-forward, everyday, family fruit cake.

8 oz flour	1 oz chopped mixed peel
4 oz butter or lard	½ teaspoon mixed spice
4 oz sugar	Pinch of salt
4 oz sultanas	1 medium egg, well beaten
4 oz raisins	¼ teaspoon bicarbonate of soda
4 oz currants	¼ pint of milk
A few slices of peel	

Set oven to 350°F or Mark 4. Well grease a 2 lb loaf tin. In a bowl, rub the fat into the flour until it resembles fine breadcrumbs. Add all the dry ingredients except the bicarbonate of soda and mix well. Slightly warm the milk in a pan and add the bicarbonate of soda. Make a well in the centre of the mixture, add the milk and the well-beaten egg and stir thoroughly together. Put the mixture into the loaf tin and arrange a few slices of peel along the top. Bake for 2 to 2½ hours until nicely brown and a skewer pushed into the centre comes out clean. Leave to stand for a few minutes and then turn out on to a wire rack to cool.

Leamingtons

A flat sponge cake topped with chocolate icing and coconut and cut into squares – a Warwickshire recipe.

2 eggs	1 teaspoon baking powder
4 oz butter	Chocolate glacé icing
4 oz caster sugar	2-3 tablespoons desiccated
4 oz flour	coconut

Set oven to 375°F or Mark 5. Grease and base-line an 8 inch square 2 inches deep cake tin. Break the eggs into a bowl set over a pan of hot water and beat lightly. In a bowl, cream the butter and sugar together then gradually beat in the eggs. Sift the flour and baking powder together and fold into the mixture. Turn the mixture into the tin and bake for 15 minutes until golden, well-risen and springy to the touch. Allow to cool in the tin, then cut into squares. Coat each square with chocolate glacé icing and sprinkle on the desiccated coconut. Makes about 9 squares.

Surrey Lardie Cakes

Sometimes known as Dough Cakes or Breakfast Cakes, these can also include caraway seeds as well as fruit and spice. Traditionally they are eaten without butter.

1 lb flour	**½ pint warm water**
1 teaspoon salt	**2 oz lard or butter**
1 oz lard	**2 oz sugar**
½ oz fresh yeast	**½ teaspoon mixed spice**
1 teaspoon caster sugar	**1 oz currants**

In a bowl, mix the flour and salt and rub in lard or butter. Cream yeast with the sugar, then stir in the water. Make a well in the flour then, when the yeast is frothy, stir it in. Mix well then turn out on to a floured surface. Knead, cover and leave in a warm place until dough has doubled in bulk. Knead again; roll out into a rectangle ¼ inch thick. Mix the sugar and spice. Spread dough with one third of fat and sprinkle on one third of sugar mixture. Fold dough into three, half turn and press edges together. Roll again. Repeat process twice more, sprinkling currants over sugar mixture the final time. Roll out and cut into 3-4 inch rounds. Score with a knife and place on a greased baking sheet. Cover and leave to rise in the warm for about 20 minutes. Set oven to 425°F or Mark 7 and bake for 25 to 30 minutes. When removed from the oven brush tops with milk while warm to give a sheen.

Guildford Castle, Surrey

Coventry Godcakes

The triangular shape of these cakes, and the three slits across the top, are said to represent the Holy Trinity, though presumably on those occasions the rum was definitely optional.

8 oz prepared puff pastry **2 teaspoons rum – optional**
4 oz mincemeat **1 egg white**
Caster sugar

Set oven to 425°F or Mark 7. Roll out the pastry thinly on a lightly floured surface and cut into 4-inch squares, then cut each square in half on the diagonal to make two triangles. Mix the mincemeat with the rum, if desired, and place spoonfuls on half of the triangles. Cover each one with another triangle, moisten the edges with a little water and press down firmly to seal. Beat the egg white lightly. Cut three slits in each cake with a very sharp knife, then brush with egg white. Sprinkle with caster sugar and place on a greased baking sheet. Bake for 15 minutes or until well risen and golden. Cool on a wire rack and eat as fresh as possible.

Spiced Oxford Cake

A dark cake containing raisins, peel, spice and treacle.

10 oz flour
½ teaspoon baking powder
¾ teaspoon mixed spice
6 oz butter
6 oz soft brown sugar

8 oz raisins or sultanas
3 oz chopped mixed peel
2 oz black treacle, warmed slightly
Juice of half a lemon
5 fl. oz. milk

Set oven to 350°F or Mark 4. Grease and base-line an 8 inch round cake tin. Sift the flour, baking powder and spice together into a bowl and then rub in the butter until the mixture resembles fine breadcrumbs. Stir in the sugar, fruit and peel. Mix the treacle and lemon juice together and stir into the mixture and then add sufficient milk to give a dropping consistency. Turn the mixture into the tin and bake for 1¾-2 hours, covering the top with a piece of kitchen foil if it appears to be browning too quickly. Allow to cool in the tin for 5 minutes, then turn out on to a wire rack.

Hereford Brandy Snaps

Originally known as 'jumbles' or 'gaufers', meaning wafers, brandy snaps were traditionally sold at fairs. These were a particular feature at the Hereford May Fair.

3 oz butter
4 oz sugar
4 oz black treacle
4 oz flour
½ teaspoon ground ginger
1 teaspoon brandy
1 teaspoon lemon juice

Melt the butter, sugar and black treacle together in a saucepan and leave to get cold. Set oven to 350°F or Mark 4. Stir the flour, ginger, brandy and lemon juice into the treacle mixture and combine very well. Drop teaspoons of the mixture on to a well-greased baking sheet and bake for 10 minutes until golden. Allow to cool slightly, then roll each one round the well-buttered handle of a wooden spoon to form 'rolls' before they set. The easiest way to do this is to bake the brandy snaps in very small batches. Allow to cool completely and serve either plain or filled with whipped cream flavoured with brandy.

Wiltshire White Cake

A pale sponge cake sandwiched with rum-flavoured whipped cream.

4 oz butter	3 egg whites
8 oz caster sugar	½ teaspoon vanilla essence or the
1 lb self-raising flour	finely grated rind of a lemon
Pinch of salt	Double cream
A scant ½ pint milk	A few drops of rum

A little sifted icing sugar

Set oven to 350°F or Mark 4. Lightly grease two 9 inch sandwich tins. Cream the butter and sugar together in a bowl. Sift the flour and salt together and add gradually, stirring between additions. Gently stir in the milk, then add the vanilla essence or lemon rind. Whisk the egg whites until they stand up in peaks and fold into the mixture. Divide the mixture between the two tins and bake for 20-30 minutes until springy to the touch. Turn out on to a wire rack and cool. Whip the cream until it holds its shape, then stir in the rum. Sandwich the cakes together with the rum-flavoured cream and dust the top lightly with sifted icing sugar.

Belvoir Castle Buns

Yeast-based buns with a filling of dried fruit, named after Belvoir Castle in Leicestershire, the family seat of the Dukes of Rutland.

1 lb flour	2 fl. oz. milk and water mixed
1 teaspoon salt	4 oz mixed currants, sultanas
2 oz butter	and chopped mixed peel
½ oz fresh yeast	Milk
4 oz caster sugar	A little extra sugar

Sift the flour and salt together into a bowl then rub in the butter. Cream the yeast into the sugar, then add the milk and water. Leave until frothy, then blend into the flour mixture, together with half the dried fruit and peel. Turn out on to a lightly floured surface and knead until the dough is smooth and elastic. Place in a clean bowl, cover and put in a warm place until the dough has risen and doubled in bulk. Knead again, lightly, for 1 minute, then roll out into a square, approximately ½-inch thick. Sprinkle on the remaining fruit and roll up like a Swiss Roll. Cut into 12 pieces, each about 1 inch thick and lay flat on a well greased baking sheet. Cover with a clean teatowel and leave to prove for about 30 minutes. Set oven to 425°F or Mark 7. Brush the buns with a little milk and sprinkle with the extra sugar. Bake for 10-15 minutes until golden brown. Cool on a wire rack.

Norfolk Vinegar Cake

This is a light farmhouse fruit cake that keeps well. Being eggless it was usually made when the hens were off lay.

8 oz butter	8 fluid oz. milk
1 lb flour	2 tablespoons cider vinegar
8 oz sugar	1 teaspoon bicarbonate
8 oz raisins	of soda, blended with
8 oz sultanas	1 tablespoon milk

Set oven to 350°F or Mark 4. Well grease and line a 9 inch round cake tin. In a bowl, rub the butter into the flour until the mixture resembles fine breadcrumbs, then stir in the sugar and the raisins and sultanas. Pour the milk into a large jug and add the cider vinegar, then stir in the bicarbonate of soda/milk mixture (you will find it will froth up.) Add to the cake mixture and stir well. Turn into the tin and bake for 30 minutes. Then reduce the oven temperature to 300°F or Mark 2 and bake for a further 1 to 1¼ hours or until a warm skewer inserted into the cake comes out clean. If the cake appears to be browning too quickly on top during cooking, cover lightly with a piece of kitchen foil. When cooked, allow the cake to cool in the tin set on a wire rack, before turning out.

Nottingham Coffee Biscuits

Round, yeast dough biscuits flavoured with caraway seeds. So called because the recipe contains 'one coffeespoon of salt'.

2 oz butter	12 oz flour
5 fl. oz milk	1 coffeespoon of salt
½ oz fresh yeast	¼ oz caraway seeds
4 oz caster sugar	1 egg, beaten

Place the butter and milk in a saucepan and warm until the butter is just melted. Cream the yeast into the sugar, stir into the butter mixture and combine well together. Sift the flour and salt together and work into the mixture, with the caraway seeds, kneading lightly until a smooth, elastic dough is formed. Cover with a clean, tea-towel and leave in a warm place until the dough has doubled in bulk. Turn the dough out on to a lightly floured surface, knead lightly and roll out to about ⅛-inch thick. Cut into round biscuits, using a 3-inch cutter. Brush liberally with beaten egg, place on a lightly greased baking sheet and prick with a fork. Leave to prove for 20 minutes. Set oven to 325°F or Mark 3 and bake the biscuits for about 30 minutes until golden in colour. Cool on a wire rack.

South Tyne Yeast Cake

Traditional to County Durham, this cake should be kept for at least a week before eating.

4 oz butter
4 oz sugar
1 egg, beaten
4 oz currants
4 oz sultanas
2 oz chopped mixed peel
¼ oz dried yeast, dissolved in 2½ fl. oz. soured milk

¼ teaspoon bicarbonate of soda, dissolved in 2½ fl. oz. cold milk
8 oz flour

FOR THE GLAZE
1 tablespoon warm milk in which 1 teaspoon of sugar has been dissolved

Well grease a 1 lb. loaf tin. Cream the butter and sugar together in a bowl until light and fluffy, then beat in the egg and stir in the fruit and peel. Add the flour, alternately with the yeast and bicarbonate of soda mixtures and combine well. Turn out on to a lightly floured surface and knead to a smooth, soft dough. Place in the tin, cover with a clean tea towel and leave in a warm place for about 30 minutes or until doubled in bulk. Set oven to 350°F or Mark 4. Bake for 2 hours, covering the top with kitchen foil if it appears to browning too quickly. Turn out of the tin, brush the top with the glaze and leave to cool on a wire rack.

Kentish Cob-nut Cake

The famous Kent Cob is not, in fact, a round cob nut, but is actually a filbert, elongated in form with a long, fringed, green husk.
It is one of the best forms of hazelnut.

8 oz self-raising flour
1 rounded teaspoon powdered ginger
4 oz margarine
4 oz brown sugar
2 oz Kentish cob-nuts, roasted and chopped (hazelnuts can be substituted, if desired)
1 large egg, beaten

Set oven to 350°F or Mark 4. Grease an approximate 9 inch x 4 inch baking tin. Sift the flour and the ginger into a bowl and rub in the margarine until the mixture resembles breadcrumbs. Add the sugar and the nuts. Mix in the beaten egg, keeping the mixture crumbly. Put the mixture into the greased tin and bake for 20 minutes. Cool in the tin and cut into squares.

Windsor Castle Cake

A cake containing ground rice and lemon rind, somewhat on the lines of a Madeira – a Berkshire recipe. The mixture is fairly sticky so, if using a loose-bottomed tin, make sure it is well lined with baking paper to seal the join.

4 oz flour
½ teaspoon baking powder
6 oz ground rice
8 oz butter
8 oz caster sugar
Grated rind of a lemon
2 eggs, beaten
½ pint milk
A little sifted icing sugar

Set oven to 350°F or Mark 4. Well grease and base line a 7 inch round cake tin. Sift the flour and baking powder together into a bowl, then add the ground rice. Rub in the butter, then stir in the sugar and lemon rind. Add the eggs, combining well, then stir in sufficient milk to produce a soft, dropping consistency. Turn into the tin and bake for 2 hours, until well-risen and golden, covering the top with a piece of baking paper if it appears to be browning too quickly. Cool in the tin for 5 minutes, then turn out and place on a wire rack. Before serving, dust the top with a little sifted icing sugar.

Shropshire Lambing Cake

A teabread containing ginger, cinnamon and dried fruit. A 'stand by' snack during lambing time.

- **4 oz margarine or butter**
- **4 oz sugar**
- **2 eggs, beaten**
- **8 oz self-raising flour**
- **2 level teaspoons mixed spice**
- **½ teaspoon cinnamon**
- **½ teaspoon ground ginger**
- **Salt**
- **2 oz sultanas or currants**
- **3 fl. oz. milk and water, mixed**

Set oven to 325°F or Mark 3. Grease and base-line a 2 lb loaf tin. Cream the fat and sugar together in a bowl until light and fluffy, then beat in the eggs, a little at a time. Sift together the flour, spices and salt and fold into the mixture, then add the fruit and sufficient liquid to produce a soft, dropping consistency. Turn the mixture into the tin and smooth the top. Bake for 20 minutes, then reduce the oven temperature to 300°F or Mark 2 for a further 40-50 minutes, covering the top with a piece of kitchen foil if it appears to be browning too quickly. Cool in the tin for 5 minutes, then turn out on to a wire rack. Serve sliced, plain or with butter.

Yorkshire Teacakes

These flat, round cakes, made with yeast dough, currants and mixed peel, are served split, toasted and buttered.

½ oz fresh yeast
½ pint tepid milk
1 lb strong white flour
1 level teaspoon salt

2 oz butter
1 oz caster sugar
4 oz currants
2 oz chopped mixed peel

Milk to glaze

Blend the yeast with a little of the tepid milk to form a creamy liquid. Place the flour and salt into a large bowl and rub in the butter. Stir in the sugar, currants and mixed peel. Make a well in the centre and add firstly the yeast cream and then sufficient of the tepid milk to make a soft but not sticky dough. Turn on to a floured surface and knead until the dough is elastic. Cover with a damp cloth and leave to rise in a warm place until doubled in bulk. Divide into eight equal pieces and knead lightly into rounds 6 inches in diameter. Place on two greased baking trays and brush with milk. Cover with a cloth and prove in a warm place until doubled in bulk. Meanwhile set oven to 400°F or Mark 6. Bake for 20 minutes until pale golden brown. Cool on a wire rack. Serve split and toasted with plenty of butter.

Knaresborough Castle, Yorkshire

Old Harry Rock Cakes

These traditional, roughly-formed 'rock-like' buns are named after the isolated chalk stacks near Studland on the Dorset coast.

8 oz. self-raising wheatmeal flour
½ teaspoon ground mixed spice
½ teaspoon ground cinnamon
4 oz butter
4 oz demerara sugar

4 oz mixed dried fruit (currants, sultanas, mixed peel, glacé cherries etc. as preferred)
Grated rind of half a lemon
1 medium egg

2 tablespoons milk

Set oven to 375°F or Mark 5. Put the flour, mixed spice and cinnamon into a bowl. Rub the butter into the dry ingredients until the mixture resembles fine breadcrumbs. Stir in the sugar, mixed dried fruits (these can be combined in any proportions as desired) and lemon rind. Add the egg and milk and combine with the dry ingredients to form a crumbly dough. Form into 10 or 12 rough heaps on a greased baking tray. Bake for approximately 20 minutes until lightly browned. Cool on the baking tray for 5 minutes before transferring to a wire rack. These rock cakes are best eaten on the same day as made. They freeze well.

Windsor Castle Cake

A cake containing ground rice and lemon rind, somewhat on the lines of a Madeira – a Berkshire recipe. The mixture is fairly sticky so, if using a loose-bottomed tin, make sure it is well lined with baking paper to seal the join.

4 oz flour	**8 oz caster sugar**
½ teaspoon baking powder	**Grated rind of a lemon**
6 oz ground rice	**2 eggs, beaten**
8 oz butter	**½ pint milk**

A little sifted icing sugar

Set oven to 350°F or Mark 4. Well grease and base line a 7 inch round cake tin. Sift the flour and baking powder together into a bowl, then add the ground rice. Rub in the butter, then stir in the sugar and lemon rind. Add the eggs, combining well, then stir in sufficient milk to produce a soft, dropping consistency. Turn into the tin and bake for 2 hours, until well-risen and golden, covering the top with a piece of baking paper if it appears to be browning too quickly. Cool in the tin for 5 minutes, then turn out and place on a wire rack. Before serving, dust the top with a little sifted icing sugar.

Bath Buns

This well-known yeast bun, originally made in the city of Bath around 1700, has a topping of coarse sugar crystals.

1 lb strong white flour	1 oz fresh yeast
½ teaspoon salt	½ pint tepid milk
2 oz butter	2 medium eggs, beaten
2 oz caster sugar	**TOPPING**
4 oz sultanas	2 oz coarse sugar
2 oz chopped mixed peel	1 beaten egg

Put the flour and salt into a large bowl and rub in the butter. Stir in the sugar, sultanas and mixed peel. Blend the yeast with a little of the tepid milk to a smooth cream. Make a well in the centre of the flour and add the yeast liquid, the beaten eggs and remaining milk and mix to a soft dough. Knead on a lightly floured surface until smooth. Place in a clean bowl, cover with a damp cloth and leave to rise in a warm place until double in size. Knock back and re-knead the dough and divide into 16 even-size pieces. Shape into rounds and place, well spaced, on to greased baking trays. Cover with a damp cloth and leave to prove in a warm place until double in size. Brush the tops with beaten egg and sprinkle with coarse sugar. Bake in a pre-heated oven 375°F or Mark 5 for 20 minutes until golden. Cool on a wire rack and serve buttered.

Gloucester Tartlets

This is a Cotswold version of Swiss Tarts.

6 oz shortcrust pastry　　**A few drops of almond essence**
2 oz butter, softened　　**1 egg, beaten**
2 oz sugar　　**2 oz ground rice**
Raspberry or apricot jam

Set oven to 375°F or Mark 5. Roll out the pastry on a lightly floured surface and use to line about 16 lightly greased and floured patty tins. In a bowl, cream the butter and sugar together, then stir in the almond essence and the egg. Fold in the ground rice and combine well. Place a little jam in each pastry case and top with a good spoonful of the ground rice mixture. Cook for 15 to 20 minutes or until the filling is golden and springy to the touch. Cool on a wire rack and before serving, dust with a little sifted icing sugar. Makes about 16 tarts.

Banbury Cakes

These oval cakes from the Oxfordshire town of Banbury date back to Tudor days, and were originally sold from special lidded baskets and wrapped in white cloths to keep them warm.

1 lb puff pastry	2 oz mixed peel
2 oz butter, melted	4 oz demerara sugar
4 oz raisins	1 level teaspoon mixed spice
4 oz currants	Egg white and caster sugar for topping

Set oven to 425°F or Mark 7. Mix the melted butter, fruit, peel, sugar and spice together in a bowl, combining well. Roll out the pastry on a lightly floured surface and, using a saucer, cut into about 16 circles. Divide the fruit mixture evenly between them, then dampen the edges of the pastry circles and draw up into the centre, sealing well. Turn over and with the hands, gently form the cakes into ovals, then press down very gently with a rolling pin. Make 3 diagonal cuts across the top of each cake, then brush with egg white and sprinke with sugar. Place on lightly greased baking trays and bake for 15 to 20 minutes or until golden. Serve slightly warm. Makes about 16 cakes.

Bury Simnel Cake

A Lancashire recipe, traditionally made for Mothering Sunday, resembling a rich curranty bread rather than the more usual marzipan-decorated fruit cake.

3 oz butter, softened
3 oz lard
1 lb self-raising flour
1 teaspoon cinnamon
1 teaspoon nutmeg
10 oz sugar
1 lb currants or 8 oz currants and 8 oz sultanas
4 oz candied peel
4 oz ground almonds
2 large eggs
A little milk

Set oven to 350°F or Mark 4. In a bowl, rub the fat into the flour until the mixture resembles fine breadcrumbs. Then stir in the spices, sugar, fruit, peel and ground almonds and combine well. Break the eggs into a bowl, combine very lightly with a fork – do not beat – and then stir into the mixture, adding a little milk, if necessary, to produce a *very* stiff dough. Grease a baking sheet and dust with flour. On a lightly floured surface, form the dough into a round and place on the baking sheet. Brush the top with milk to glaze. Bake for about 50 to 60 minutes, or until a skewer inserted into the cake comes out clean. Cool on a wire rack. As Bury Simnel Cake is not confined to a tin, the dough *must* be stiff enough to hold its shape during cooking, but be prepared for it to spread a little.

Devonshire Cider Cake

Devon, with its neighbouring county of Somerset, is renowned for its home-made cider which gives this cake its distinctive flavour.

4 oz caster sugar **8 oz self-raising flour**
4 oz butter **1 teaspoon cinnamon**
2 medium eggs **½ pint cider**

Set oven to 350°F or Mark 4. Grease and line an 8 inch round cake tin. Cream the sugar and butter together in a bowl until pale in colour. Stir in the eggs, cinnamon and half of the flour. Gradually add the cider to this mixture and lastly add the remaining flour and mix thoroughly. Pour into the tin and bake for approximately 45 minutes until firm to the touch and golden in colour.

Beach Huts - Dawlish

Brighton Gingerbread

This traditional, light gingerbread is from the Prince Regent's favourite Sussex sea-side resort.

6 oz butter	**1 teaspoon mixed spice**
6 oz caster sugar	**1 teaspoon ground ginger**
3 eggs	**Scant ½ teaspoon baking powder**
3 oz black treacle	**2-4 oz flaked almonds**
8 oz flour	**3 tablespoons milk**

Set oven to 350°F or Mark 4. Line an 8 inch square cake tin. In a bowl, cream the butter and sugar and add the eggs, beating them in well. Sift all the dry ingredients together and fold into the creamed mixture with the treacle. Fold in the almonds and milk. Pour into the prepared tin and bake for about ¾ hour until firm.

Staffordshire Fruit Cake

A rich fruit cake recipe which includes black treacle and brandy.

6 oz butter	2 oz black treacle
6 oz caster sugar	2 oz ground almonds
4 eggs	8 oz currants
8 oz flour	2 oz glacé cherries, quartered
½ teaspoon ground mace	2 oz chopped mixed peel
½ teaspoon baking powder	1 tablespoon brandy

1 dessertspoon lemon juice

Set oven to 350°F or Mark 4. Grease and line an 8 inch round cake tin. Cream the butter and sugar together in a bowl until light and fluffy. Whisk the eggs together in a bowl set over a pan of hot water, then beat into the butter mixture. Sift together the flour, mace and baking powder and fold into the butter mixture, alternately with the treacle and ground almonds. Mix the currants, cherries and peel together and stir into the mixture with the brandy and lemon juice. Turn the mixture into the prepared tin and smooth over the top. Bake for 2 hours, covering the top with a piece of kitchen foil if it appears to be browning too quickly. Allow to cool in the tin for 5 minutes, then turn out on to a wire rack.

METRIC CONVERSIONS

The weights, measures and oven temperatures used in the preceding recipes can be easily converted to their metric equivalents.

Weights

Avoirdupois	Metric
1 oz.	just under 30 grams
4 oz. (¼ lb.)	app. 115 grams
8 oz. (½ lb.)	app. 230 grams
1 lb.	454 grams

Liquid Measures

Imperial	Metric
1 tablespoon (liquid only)	20 millilitres
1 fl. oz.	app. 30 millilitres
1 gill (¼ pt.)	app. 145 millilitres
½ pt.	app. 285 millilitres
1 pt.	app. 570 millilitres
1 qt.	app. 1.140 litres

Oven Temperatures

	°Fahrenheit	Gas Mark	°Celsius
Slow	300	2	140
	325	3	158
Moderate	350	4	177
	375	5	190
	400	6	204
Hot	425	7	214
	450	8	232
	500	9	260

Flour as specified in these recipes refers to Plain Flour unless otherwise described.